Meditations on the Twelve Holy Nights

The journey between Christmas Eve on December 24 and Epiphany Eve on January 5

Kristina Kaine

Copyright © 2016 Kristina Kaine

I AM Press

All rights reserved.

ISBN-13: 978-1539838005

ISBN-10: 1539838005

Cover designed by Adriana Koulias
Cover artwork: Lorenzo di Credi: Birth of Christ

Meditations on the Twelve Holy Nights

License Notes
This book is licensed to you for your personal use. Please do not photocopy. Out of respect for the author, if you would like to share it with another person please purchase an additional copy for each recipient.

Written during the Holy Nights each year between 2011 and 2016
Published on Face Book and on www.esotericconnection.com

This book is written from the insight of the author, if similar information is found in other books this is co-incidental. Quotes by other authors are referenced.

More information about the author's other works and websites is listed at the end of this book.

DEDICATION

To all those who read words of wisdom with love in their hearts.

CONTENTS

	Acknowledgments	i
	Background	ii
	Indications given by Rudolf Steiner	v
1	Holy Night One	1
2	Holy Night Two	5
3	Holy Night Three	10
4	Holy Night Four	15
5	Holy Night Five	20
6	Holy Night Six	25
7	Holy Night Seven	30
8	Holy Night Eight	35
9	Holy Night Nine	40
10	Holy Night Ten	45
11	Holy Night Eleven	50
12	Holy Night Twelve	55
13	Holy Night Thirteen – Epiphany	61
	Author's Other Work	64

ACKNOWLEDGMENTS

Special thanks to Laura Zanutto who acquired the original German text in 2015 and translated it using Google. Also for translating the meditations into Italian each year. Thank you also to Miriam Petri for your translations into Hebrew. Gratitude to Adriana Koulias for the beautiful cover.

THE HOLY DAYS AND NIGHTS

Introduction

The Holy Days and Nights is the period between Christmas Eve, which celebrates the birth of Jesus (described by Luke) and January 6th which is called Epiphany, which celebrates the baptism of Jesus in the Jordan by John the Baptist.

This period is like the germinating seed in the depths of the earth which will sprout and finally bloom at the Resurrection of the Christ-ened Jesus after the crucifixion.

During these days and nights we have the opportunity to reach a new level of understanding of this, the most profound mystery known to man, and indeed in the whole universe.

This book contains short contemplations written between 2011-12 and 2015-16 during the Holy Days and Nights. These contemplations are based on indications given by Rudolf Steiner to one of his pupils, Herbert Hahn*, for the twelve Holy Nights - twelve because that ties them to the twelve months of the year. There are in fact Thirteen Holy Days and Nights which Rudolf Steiner spoke of in 1911, quoted below.

In 2015 Laura Zanutto acquired the original German text and translated it using Google, which was then adjusted by Laura and tweaked by Kristina Kaine.

*Bibliography of Herbert Hahn https://en.wikipedia.org/wiki/Herbert_Hahn

What Rudolf Steiner said about these days and nights

For one whose eyes of spirit are opened, the Thirteen Days and Thirteen Nights between the 24th of December and the 6th of January are a time of deep spiritual experience. Parallel with the experience of the plant-seed in the depths of the natural earth, there is a spiritual experience in the earth's spirit-depths — verily a parallel experience. And the seer for whom this experience is possible either as the result of training or through inherited clairvoyant faculties, can feel himself penetrating into these spiritual depths. During this period of the Thirteen Days and Nights, the seer can behold what must come upon man because he has passed through incarnations which have been under the influence of the forces of Lucifer since the beginning of earthly evolution.

The sufferings in Kamaloca that man must endure in the spiritual world because Lucifer has been at his side since he began to incarnate on the earth — the dearest vision of all this is presented in the mighty Imaginations which can come before the soul during the Thirteen Days and Nights between the Christmas Festival and the Festival of the 6th of January, the Epiphany.

At the time when the seed of the plant is passing through its most crucial period in the depths below, the human soul is passing through its deepest experiences. The soul gazes at a vista of all that man must experience in the spiritual worlds because, under Lucifer's influence, he alienated himself from the Powers by whom the world was created.

This vision is clearest to the soul during these Thirteen Days and Nights. Hence there is no better preparation for the revelation of that Imagination which may be called the Christ Imagination and which makes us aware that by gaining the victory over Lucifer, Christ Himself becomes the Judge of the deeds of men during the incarnations affected by Lucifer's influence. The soul of the seer lives on from the festival of Jesus' birth to that of the Epiphany in such a way that the Christ Mystery is revealed. It is during these Thirteen Holy Days and Nights that the soul can grasp most deeply of all, the import and meaning of the Baptism by John in the

Jordan. The Birth of the Sun-Spirit as the Spirit of the Earth by Rudolf Steiner, Hanover, 26th December, 1911 The full lecture is available at www.rsarchive.com

Using the contemplations throughout the year

The twelve Holy Nights sow a seed in our soul for our progress through the year ahead. Our sole purpose on this earth is to become aware our I Am, our True Self. By applying each of the twelve Holy Nights to each of the twelve months throughout the year we come closer to knowing ourselves more completely. In its highest expression our I Am unites with Christ who accompanies us each step of the way.

"The true name of Christ is "I Am"; who does not know or does not understand this and calls Him by another name does not know anything about Him. "I Am" is His only name." Rudolf Steiner 27 May 1909

Indications given by Rudolf Steiner to Herbert Hahn for the Twelve Holy Nights

On December 24th the twelve Holy Nights begin.

The twelve Holy Nights are symbols for the twelve forces of the soul that live in us. And so this indication is valid forever, not only for the twelve Holy Nights.

On January 1 at noon we have the Sun as close as possible to the Earth and that is why there are just five and half days before and five and a half days later, which is the time of the twelve Holy Nights.

On these nights, the darkest of the year, we are closest to the Sun's Spirit and this means that the Spiritual Sun shining from inside the Earth makes it translucent and illuminates everything from the inside, not as it is afterwards when the Sun illuminates the Earth from above, from the outside.

You have to enter these twelve Holy Nights wide awake and very conscious. It is important that the first night (December 24th) we only stay awake until one or two in the morning. On the other nights, if possible, try to go to bed regularly at the same time, it is of principal importance to live in a regular rhythm at this time, if this is not possible in the active life, one has to try to do so internally. Those who cannot be silent in the external life should seek constantly to be inwardly aware of the sanctity of the time. It is important to perform daily duties without losing sight of this realization, of the sacredness of the time, allowing nothing unhealthy, no ugly movement to enter the soul, remaining always attentive and severe on oneself in this regard.

During the experience of Christmas, with its twelve Holy Nights, we sow the seed for the next twelve months. Therefore these twelve days are important, if for example we make mistakes on the first day, we lay a seed, which, in the first month, will germinate negatively in the blood.

We must try to pass the twelve Holy Days properly, according to the Law, because we need each year to work on our rebirth and we cannot lose any year.

HOLY NIGHT ONE
24-25 December

Christmas Eve, when Christ is born in the soul, the soul asks: can I listen with all my weaknesses, deficiencies and passions?

Symbol: The stable of Bethlehem, in which in lowliness and poverty is born the Light of the World. The Voice of the Silence penetrates to the soul and teaches to affirm joyfully the good in us and others.

Capricorn. The Divine Spirit is born in Matter. Spirit and Matter, the Alpha and Omega touches and creates life.

Mystery: The seeking soul in the darkness of a trackless forest. Rudolf Steiner

1. Heilige Nacht in Bezug auf Januar
24./25. Dezember – Steinbock

Der Heilige Abend, an dem Christus der Seele geboren wird. Und die Seele fragt: kann ich mit all meinen Schwächen und Mängeln und Leidenschaften erhört werden? Symbol: Der Stall von Bethlehem, in dessen Niedrigkeit und Armut wurde das Licht der Welt hineingeboren. Die Stimme der Stille dringt zur Seele und lehrt sie, das Gute in uns und den Anderen freudig zu bejahen. Steinbock. Göttlicher Geist wird im Stoff geboren. Geist und Stoff, das A und O berühren sich und es entsteht Leben.

Mysterium: die suchende Seele im Dunkel eines weglosen Waldes. Rudolf Steiner

Contemplations for the first night by Kristina Kaine

In the humble stable of our soul a child is born who will change the world. Why would our soul be such a place? The stable was the only place available for the very pregnant Mary. This was the resting place for the animals that, on the one hand, are part of nature providing our sustenance, but on the other hand represent our astral nature that does what it wants unless it is trained.

Pause and focus with reverence on your soul. Consider the gifts of feeling, thinking and will that are at our disposal. See them lying in your soul for you to open and use as you so desire. Feel a deep thankfulness for this. What would life be if we could not feel the beauty in this world, and the beauty of the souls around us? What would life be if we could not connect ideas together to make sense of our lives? What would life be if we could not direct our behaviour appropriately? At this time we can also pour out our hearts to those who cannot use these gifts fully. The intensity of our compassion fills the universe with Christmas lights. 2011

~ ~ ~

Do we dare look at the darkness of our soul? The dark thoughts, the gloomy feelings and our weak and indecisive will? This is our stable. We live in a world that would usher us into the glamorous inn and hide the stable away from us. If we allow this to happen our I Am will not be born in our soul.

Our I Am is the Alpha and Omega; it existed in the beginning and we give birth to it at the end. This is our purpose; it is part of who we are. We can only fathom the mystery by engaging with our I Am; which is why the "soul seeks the mystery in a dark and trackless forest." It is dark because we do not shine the light of our I Am in our soul, and because we avoid going there it is trackless. If we have the courage to go to the stable we will give birth to who we really are. The stable is our life here on this earth. If we can accept this, and look into our dark soul with the light of our I Am, the difficulties in our soul will disappear just like magic. Then we have nothing to fear. 2012

~ ~ ~

Are we worthy to participate in this birth? Perhaps that is why the Christ Child was born in a humble stable to remind us that it is okay to welcome this birth in our soul, even though we are very aware of our weaknesses, flaws and passions. They are part of who we are, they are the challenges that strengthen us as we overcome them. Each tiny victory is a step forward in the dark and trackless forest. No one can lead us, we must make our own way. We must quell the fear and find the courage to accept that a miracle is born within us this night.

It is said that this child could speak at birth. If we can quieten all feelings of unworthiness and know that we have this precious gift within us, we will hear this voice. It is a voice of silence because no words are necessary to know the joy of goodness. The goodness in ourselves that is utterly worthy to hold this new life within us. The joy of goodness that we also see in others as they struggle with their own feelings of worthiness. In this way we assist each other to feel worthy. 2013

~ ~ ~

This is the night we are shown the mystery of who we really are. Do we dare to look upon the dazzling purity of the Christ child? The angels surround us to give us the courage and immediately we realize how far we are from this perfection. Yet it is this experience of powerlessness that awakens us so that we can hear the reassuring voice of silence.

No matter how small and insignificant we feel we can know with all certainty that Christ lives within our soul. As we contemplate the infant in the manger so we are contemplating our own soul in all its glory. The child waits for us to acknowledge his presence within us. In fact, we could ask if he has really been born at all if we do not acknowledge him in our soul in every moment of our lives. Whatever we face in life, whatever encounters we have, we can be sure that Christ is within us and within everyone we meet.

This Divine Spirit is born in matter and dwells here like a seed; the Alpha and Omega, the first and the last.

Through the twelve Holy Nights we plant the seeds for the coming year. May this holy birth be a reality in each one of us, and if so, we will change the world as He did over 2000 years ago. 2014

~ ~ ~

How do we listen to the Voice of Silence? Listening is a special gift which becomes more attuned lifetime after lifetime as we are able to hear the Voice of Silence. If we have difficulty physically hearing the noises in our world in this life it can point to the way in which we listened in past lives. The same applies to any inability to hear the truth today.

We can never listen while we underestimate who we are. This is when the chatter of our weaknesses, deficiencies and passions drowns out the Voice of Silence. What is this Voice of Silence? It is the Logos, the Creative Word that speaks loudly, silently and continuously creating this Universe. If we can listen to it we can co-create with it.

The task of the Creative Word was *"To place the future of mankind and earth in the hands of human beings and not interfere through a divine word of command - what confidence in man is that!"* Hans-Werner Schroeder, The Cosmic Christ

The Christ Child is born tonight to remind us of this gift of freedom. Through this gift we become creators, initially creating our own Self through our ability to listen to the Voice of Silence. 2015

HOLY NIGHT TWO
December 25-26 - Aquarius

Night of John. The Eagle of the soul circling high on its wings and looking back from a great height, observes its own life. And now the man recognizes the Laws of Karma.

The Mystery: Choosing the narrow and difficult path or the path that is wide and easy.

For those who are born of flesh it is hard to find the path of the spirit.

Bhagavad Gita: A selfish life, or a life devoted to humanity? Rudolf Steiner

2. Heilige Nacht
25.-26. Dezember – Wassermann

Nacht des Johannes. Der Adler der Seele kreist hoch auf seinen Schwingen, schaut zurück aus grosser Höhe und betrachtet sein eigenes Leben. Und jetzt erkennt der Mensch die Gesetze des Karma.

Das Mysterium: Den schmalen und schwierigen Pfad oder den breiten und einfachen Weg wählen. Für den, der aus dem Fleische geboren ist, ist es schwer den Pfad des Geistes zu finden.

Bhagavad Gita: Ein eigennütziges Leben, oder ein der Menschheit gewidmetes Leben? Rudolf Steiner

Contemplations for the second night by Kristina Kaine

Christmas is a spiritually elevating time which can sometimes clash with the materialistic ideas of the modern world. We must strike the delicate balance between experiencing our spiritual self and our earthly self. We are inclined to clothe our spiritual self in our earthly understanding thereby masking its beauty and purity. Our task is to integrate the two by always acknowledging that our spiritual self underpins our earthly self.

When we look at our lives through the eyes of our spiritual self we see how we attract all our difficulties for the express purpose of making us stronger and more objective. For it is only with objectivity that we can even see our spiritual self, our I Am. Christ came to earth to give us personal use of our I Am, that is the real Christmas gift. Do we reject it? Yes, we do. Each time we blame others for what they do to us we reject this gift. We only ever accept this gift when we acknowledge that whatever happens to us we have attracted so that we can experience this gift more fully. If we can become the interested observer of all that takes place in our lives we stand with Christ and share his work. 2011

~ ~ ~

How can we get far enough away from ourselves to see the big picture of our own biography? Only on eagle's wings! The eagle is the one that can fly the highest. From that vantage point we can see how our life plays out as we planned it before we incarnated.

Our life is like lifting weights; we put as many weights on the bar as we need to build our strength. Of course we groan, but at the same time we have our eyes on the plan. The plan is to become a self-realised individual not relying on other people or gods. In this way we become self-reliant I Am beings.

If we could look at every single encounter in our life with this attitude, the narrow and difficult path would at the same time be wide and easy. Then we truly know that the goal is to love as John the Beloved loved and was loved. As we experience our own difficulties we know that every other person also has difficulties.

Why would we speak harshly to them? Why would we criticise them? Why would we think thoughts about them that we would not dare to speak to them?

If we can take the eagle's perspective we feel compassion for each and every soul playing out their own biography? We will also feel compassion for ourselves. Then we stand with Buddha who saw behind the superficial illusion to the reality of each person's true identity. 2012

~ ~ ~

This night we celebrate John who was initiated by Christ himself. He was a forerunner for our evolutionary development. His symbol is the eagle, the one who did not enter fully into matter and who soars in the etheric spheres of this earth. Here we have the image of sense-free thinking; thinking that soars above earthly restrictions to reveal spiritual truth. If we have the love of John and the mobility in the etheric of the eagle, we see the true purpose of karma.

Our karma is a gift, it is only through our karma that we can experience freedom. It is the eagle who reminds us that we can be free. Yet mostly we think of karma as a punishment because of the great pain it causes in our soul. It is our choice to experience karma as pain, or as joy for the freedom it brings. If we experience it as pain then it contracts our being into the narrow and difficult path. If we experience it as joy we recognise karma as the redemption of man by himself.

When we release ourselves from the difficulty of our karma then our karma becomes a sacrament. This act of freeing ourselves creates a substance that flows from our hearts into the hearts of others. It is our selflessness that creates this substance. It is born out of harmony; harmony that we choose to restore by refusing to engage in our karma at that level which can create great disharmony for ourselves and others. Then through the eyes of love we see the infant who will become the Lord of Karma. 2013

~ ~ ~

The Night of John means the Night of Love, for John is Love. What greater love is there than the love for the child in our soul? John saw this, he didn't see his earthly short comings. To see our shortcomings is to be overwhelmed by our karma which defeats it's purpose.

How do we see the spiritual in us, in others, and in everything? The artist Sigmund Gleismüller had deep insight when he painted John gazing at Mary-Sophia while grounded in the physical world accompanied by his symbol the eagle. This Imagination teaches us how to Imagine the spiritual reality in us and around us.

Through our Imagination we can achieve the perspective of the eagle and then we will gaze on our own life as if we were viewing someone else's life. We become lovingly objective and compassionate. This reminds us that spiritual beings accompanying us every step of the way. If we don't do this we are born of flesh. Flesh becomes the reality as it disguises the spirit. We forget that we are beings of spirit and soul - our flesh is simply our cloak.

When we step into the living Imagination that reveals to us that we are beings of soul and spirit we enter into a new reality. We value every person me meet. We stop looking at their physical appearance, their clothes and their physical expressions - which is simply the cloak of their karma, and we begin to see their spirit. When we see a person's spirit they are changed. They feel recognised for who they truly are. We could even say that unless we see the spirit, it remains hidden. Seeing the spirit in each other means that we are devoted to humanity in all it's potential. 2014

~ ~ ~

The child is born in our soul sending the Eagle into flight. From this great height we become aware of the Eagle and all that it represents. As the dove brings the seed of the Holy Spirit into our being, the Eagle draws us to the heights of Intuition. Intuition is not a sixth sense, not a psychic instinct; Intuition is the highest human faculty of knowledge. Through it we experience the Word which St John tells us was in the beginning. John knows this Word because he is the first human being to hear it resound silently within him.

We all experience Intuition, consciously or unconsciously. We experience it when we surrender ourselves and enter into others. Are we up for this? Can we enter into another person's pain and recognize the Laws of Karma playing out within them? We can't if we are absorbed in our own karma. We have to step out of our own karma as we would step out of a tent, and not only step out of the tent but also step out of it naked, like a newborn.

In this condition we can enter purely into the other person and truly know them. Of course, they have to be willing to allow this to take place. It is this union that gives us the ability to soar like an Eagle and circle at a great height. From this perspective we see the overview, but also with the eye of the Eagle we see every minute detail. In this way we become devoted to humanity, not sentimentally but with true knowledge and great compassion. 2015

HOLY NIGHT THREE
December 26-27 - Pisces

The three nights of the white lily.

The soul recognizes that it is unable to hold above, that it is drawn down again, because there is so much earthly weight in it.

The soul begins consciously to purify the earthly body as it looks at every meal as "Holy Viaticum (communion)": "I am the bread"

"We come from the bread, we live out of bread along the way of formation and return to the bread."

    Mystery: Never forget the goal of goals in the long walks in the earthly realm. Rudolf Steiner

    3. Heilige Nacht
    26./27.– Fische
    Die drei Nächte der weissen Lilie.

    Die Seele erkennt, dass sie sich nicht oben zu halten vermag, dass sie wieder hinunter gezogen wird, weil noch soviel Erdenhaftes in ihr ist. Die Seele schickt sich bewusst an, den irdischen Körper zu reinigen, indem sie jede Speise gleichsam als "Heilige Wegzehrung" ansieht:

    "Ich bin das Brot .."

    "Wir kommen aus dem Brot, leben auf dem Entwickungweg aus dem Brot und kehren zurück in das Brot."

    Mysterium: Nie das Ziel der Ziele vergessen bei den weiten Wanderungen im Erdriech. R. Steiner

Contemplations for the third night by Kristina Kaine

When we have spiritual insight we see that we are really part of the All. Then we are tempted to see ourselves as part of the All regardless of what we do. This choice means that we stand still on our journey and have some kind of faith that we will get there one day. However, we need also to use this spiritual insight to see the baggage that we carry; not to do so is a misuse of this spiritual ability. We don't want to look at the baggage because we think that if we look at it we won't have the strength to sift through it.

So what is the baggage? Our grudges, our lack of forgiveness, our fear, our lack of love, our opinions, our one-sidedness, our jealousy, undervaluing ourselves, overvaluing ourselves, the list goes on. This baggage belongs to our lower self, our lower ego which found the strength to develop itself in all these things. Now that we have come within reach of our higher self, our I Am, which is the bread of life, we no longer have use for these things. In fact now we need the exact opposite of these things. Leaving aside our opinions gives us the freedom to see much, much more. Loving others as they are is so much easier than deciding who to love and who not to love. While we may not experience instant gratification from forgiving others, when we forgive we change the world. 2011

~ ~ ~

The lily symbolises the soul which finds its Higher Self, its I Am. This is the work that we have undertaken. We do this work in our ordinary everyday lives; in our activities but also in our thoughts and feelings. In this way we purify our soul and assist it to regain its virginal status. The I Am can only be born of a virgin who has regained her virginity.

This birth always involves death, death to all that is impure. This is why the lily is associated with death because with every death comes new life. This process of death and rebirth takes place perpetually in our soul. Irritating feelings can be replaced in a flash; they die and are replaced by new feelings. The same with judgemental thoughts and selfish motives; not that we shouldn't have them but that we are able to exercise control over them at will. This is the freedom that comes with our I Am. We are free to choose to feel, think and act in whatever way we like.

Each time we think bad thoughts about people we misuse our freedom. Furthermore, we take away their freedom to be who they are. It is love, the love of the virgin soul for its I Am-child, that brings with it true freedom.

Then we know that the I Am is the bread, the only form of nourishment that we need. At the same time, bread, which is our most basic food, enables us to live on this earth thereby making it possible for us integrate our I Am – we have to do it here. This is the distant objective that we are working towards. If we do not integrate our I Am humanity has no future. Much depends on us. 2012

~ ~ ~

The Christ child can only be born in the purest of pure. We came from purity, a purity that was bestowed on us by the finest spiritual forces. The lily is a symbol of this purity. The lily stands there to remind us of our source and assure us that we can return to it. Every thing in this world speaks to us of a spiritual truth. Each thing touches our senses in a such a way that unconsciously we know the mysteries of the universe. This is like the comfort and reassurance of a mother from which we are born.

When we look at the lily we experience ourselves as something separate from it. We are here, it is over there. It is this experience that makes us conscious of ourselves. Otherwise we are unaware of ourselves and our potential.

Our task is to understand why we are separate from all that we see, then out of our own understanding to see that we are not separate at all. In the meantime, the experience of separation innately involves the experience of fear. To meet this fear with courage we need our I Am, the highest human element that reconnects us to our purity. The whole purpose of the birth of the Christ child was to give us a personal connection with our I Am. 2013

~ ~ ~

What value do we place on our food? Do we eat to satisfy the craving to eat? Or do we eat with reverence so that we build the vessel, the form, that houses our soul and spirit making it possible for us to live on this earth? If we think about it, all external things are none other than the human body because we take them into us and through an alchemical process we transform them into our body. Through this process we kill nature and resurrect its life-force to build and sustain our physical form. This, and only this, makes it possible for us to experience our I Am. This is the purpose of our physical life; we incarnate in the flesh and through our own individual effort experience the fourth human element, the I Am.

This means that we can only be physical human beings because we take into ourselves what nature provides. The bread we consume and transform becomes our flesh, if we have no bread we have no flesh. If we have a loaf of bread and we share it with a friend then we are sharing our flesh with them. If we had eaten it, it would have become our flesh. Is this what Christ was showing us when he said I Am the bread? Is this what he revealed at the Last Supper - take and eat for this is my body, take this wine, it is my blood?

If Christ had eaten that piece of bread or taken that sip of wine it would have become his body, but in a loving gesture he gave it to us so that it may become our body thereby creating a bond. Perhaps he was also showing his appreciation, and therefore reverence, for being able to enter fully into a body of flesh that he made the bread and the wine a symbol of his death in the body and resurrection in the spirit as he left the earthly realm.

Based on ideas from "Seeing Christ in Sickness and Healing" by Peter Selg quoting Paracelsus. 2014

~ ~ ~

If we cannot know our soul we cannot know Christ. It is as simple as that. Every thought, feeling and action taking place in our soul has weight and it is up to us to measure it. Think of a set of scales, are the weights too heavy on the earthly side or the spiritual side? Our task is to balance them by taking off, or adding on weight to the side which is out of balance.

The weight of this world can lay heavily in our heart and we can long for the freedom of spirit. Yet, freedom is a choice. We can choose freedom whenever we wish here on this earth. We have the god-like ability to change our attitude in the twinkling of an eye. It is when we see the true goal, which is to transform ourselves into the bread, the body of Christ, that we have real power to change our attitude.

Because of this it is up to us to see everything we eat as Holy Communion. It is through the food we eat that we have the opportunity to connect with our I Am. If the food supply of the earth is disrupted it is a sign that we eat our food without full consideration its Holy source; this earth which is the body of Christ. As we eat each mouthful we must consider the earth from which the food has grown, the warmth of the sun that nourished its growth, and our fellow human beings who made it possible for the food to be on our plate. This is, of course, the purpose behind the tradition of saying grace. In this way, mouthful by mouthful, we will purify our soul and body. 2015

HOLY NIGHT FOUR
December 27-28 - Aries

Consciously purify the Astral Body: antipathy and sympathy are converted into universal love. Passions and desires keep silent.

The power of Christ penetrates with his light and his strength what is Luciferic in us.

Mystery: The work on ourselves serves the best interests of the whole. The Archangel Uriel holds up a mirror in which we see ourselves as we are. Rudolf Steiner

4. Heilige Nacht

27./28. – Widder

Bewusst den Astralkörper reinigen: Antipathie und Sympathie wird in All-Liebe umgewandelt. Leidenschaften und Begierden schweigen. Die Christuskraft durchleuchtet und durchkraftet in uns, was luziferisch ist.

Mysterium: Die Arbeit an uns selbst dient dem Wohl des Ganzen. Der Erzengel Uriel hält uns den Spiegel vor, in dem wir sehen, wie wir sind. Rudolf Steiner

Contemplations for the fourth night by Kristina Kaine

Even though we have three soul forces; Sentient / feeling soul, Mind / thinking soul and Consciousness / willing soul, our overall soul mood is centred in our feeling activities. Our basic experience of feeling in our soul draws us to what we like and what we dislike, to sympathy and antipathy, or love and hate.

If we think about our own disposition we can understand ourselves quite clearly if we observe what we accept and what we reject, what we are drawn to and what repels us. Some say that this is influenced by our upbringing but essentially it can be directly linked to our karma and our experiences from past lives.

So we are attracted to everything that pleases us and we ignore everything else. This means that a large part of this world passes us by unnoticed, as if it didn't exist. This has a damaging effect on us and prevents us from engaging with our Higher Self and awaking the presence of Christ within us. 2011

~ ~ ~

How strange it is that human beings have an astral body but most people are not really aware of it. As children, when we said that we were hungry, our mothers didn't say to us, "That is your astral body telling you that your physical body needs foods." Or, if we said that we were tired, she didn't say, "That is your astral body loosening." If we can introduce these ideas into our thinking then we will be much more in touch with our astral body.

With this awareness we will experience our semi-conscious habit of feeling sympathy and antipathy – but let's call it what it really is: love and hate. If we react to the harshness of the word hate then that is the antipathy of our astral. Even love can be astral sympathy. If we are to refine our astral responses, we need to rise above this automatic response of like and dislike, acceptance and rejection.

The love that silences passions and desires is unbiased, it doesn't love because … . This love, agape, sees deeply into the other person and finds Christ as he dwells within each person since Golgotha. This creates a kind of chain reaction. When something is seen that has remained unnoticed it stirs, it becomes active, like the lily rising out of its bulb. It is as if we activate Christ within each other by silently acknowledging his presence within us.

Then we have the courage to look into Uriel's mirror and see ourselves as we really are. What do we see? Christ! All our shortcomings fall into perspective. We see that they are a necessary part of our biography and with this understanding we will love ourselves. Loving ourselves brings out our love for others. Then the tempters, Ahriman and Lucifer, can do their job – we will feel them tugging at our astral as sympathy and antipathy and in this way giving us the opportunity to resist them. As we see them playing their game, and we refuse to play we give rise to our metamorphosis. 2012

~ ~ ~

How do we find Christ within us? How do we experience the presence of this Cosmic being who came to show us complete love? The one who enlightens and fortifies us. How do we get over all the religious ideas that have seeped into our being over the last two thousand years to find the real Christ? One of the most potent ideas spoken by Rudolf Steiner is to experience powerlessness.

What is it within us that hates to feel powerless? Our astral, our lower soul levels, our survival instinct that wants to prevail. In our astral being we are polarised between what we like and what we dislike. This region of our being is ruled by feelings not balanced by thinking, and feelings acting like will forces which is when we can react to things that we dislike. So how do we overcome this? One way to purify our astral is to listen to the other person's point of view, in so doing we put ourselves in a powerless position and we don't object to what they are saying.

In this way we hold up Uriel's mirror and the other person will see who they are themselves. They will see whether they speak the truth or not. This is love, pure and selfless love coming from our Higher Self, our I Am. Through these I Am forces Christ is revealed in our soul. After we truly experience the powerlessness we then experience the resurrection from powerlessness and that is when we find Christ within us. That is when we have a genuine experience of his presence within us. 2013

~ ~ ~

Do we really know what love is? Most of the time we love because it suits us, and we hate because it suits us. This love is biased and rooted in the karma arising out of our past-life experiences. True love can only be experienced when we love another person regardless.

Strange as it is, love can often arise out of hatred. When we strongly disagree with something or someone, we join forces with those who share our disagreement. We feel united with them in our 'cause' as we oppose the ideas and actions of the other person. It is easy to think that we are right, that we are united in love for those in the group who agree with our cause, but, in fact, we are really motivated by a lack of love.

To experience true love we begin by thinking love rather than feeling it. Feeling-love arises in our astral body, thinking-love is a spiritual act arising out of mental picturing. It is through the strength of our mental picturing that we can truly love Christ and in this same way love each other.

When we are able to love another person in this pure way, with no ulterior motive, they are transformed and become more loving in their own lives. This is the secret behind the New Commandment in the Gospel of St John. "A new commandment I give to you, that you love one another; even as I have loved you, that you also love one another." John 13:34

One of the reasons we find it so hard to love others purely is because pure love is so intense that we can be fearful of it. This is why it is so important for us to learn to love Christ through the process of mental picturing. He then gives us the strength and courage to love ourselves as we are, and to love others as they are. 2014

~ ~ ~

How often do we think about the impact of our personal development on the universe? How could a seemingly insignificant human being such as ourselves affect this enormous universe? This idea is expressed in the notion of the "Butterfly Effect."

While we can't know for sure if the flap of one butterfly's wing on one side of the world causes a storm on the other side of the world, the negativity of many human beings in a room is palpable. If this is the case, imagine the effect on another person of our antipathy towards them. Antipathy is usually accompanied by criticism and if we freely engage in this behaviour we are a long way from purifying our astral body - even if we think the other person deserves it.

When we unconsciously exercise our sympathy and antipathy we invite Lucifer into our consciousness. Lucifer always degrades our experiences and causes us to focus on ourselves. Lucifer causes selfishness in our astral body, lying in our etheric body, and illness in our physical body. If we become aware of the ways in which we like one thing and dislike another, and try to rise above these instincts, Lucifer's activity will be exposed.

Lucifer has a rightful place within us, but only as a catalyst for change in our consciousness. He is not there to use our consciousness as his own playing field. As long as we do not resist him, and unwittingly play along with his often mischievous ideas, our astral will be murky. When we start to observe his activity it is a signal to the power of Christ to become active within us like the sun shining through the clouds. If enough people do this it will have a powerful effect on the whole universe. 2015

HOLY NIGHT FIVE
December 28-29 - Taurus

Consciously purify the body of thought. Discipline thinking. Concentrating on the positive. Converting the black doves of thought into white doves, because our thinking is, until it is not consciously conducted with discipline, like a dovecote! This dovecote also [keep] closed against foreign, negative thoughts.

Mystery: The purification of the temple by Jesus Christ. Rudolf Steiner

5. Heilige Nacht
28./29. – Stier

Bewusst den Gedankenkörper reinigen. Gedankenzucht. Konzentration auf Positives. Umwandeln der schwarzen Gedankentauben in weiße, denn unser Denken gleicht, solange es nicht bewusst in Zucht genommen wird, einem Taubenschlag! Diesen Taubenschlag auch schließen vor fremden, negativen Gedanken.

Mysterium: Die Tempelreinigung durch Jesus-Christus. Rudolf Steiner

Contemplations for the fifth night by Kristina Kaine

When we think, we combine concepts developed in the past to make sense of the present. We do not do this in our brain. Our brain is like a mirror so that we can see the thoughts that are formed by our soul; so it is our soul that sends our thoughts to our body. This is why we can't think when we are asleep, our soul /astral being has withdrawn (but our brain is still there in the bed and scientists have all sorts of notions about why it doesn't work at night – except the right one!)

So how much control do we have over these thoughts? 100%! All we need is to sharpen our concentration. If we are able to concentrate on our thinking, it, and we, will be transformed. We will experience thinking like a breath of inspiration, it will be freed from its predictable and tedious ways and we will feel liberated. We will have direct control to warm up our thoughts with feeling and bring our thinking to life with our will. This will give us a direct experience of our I Am which isn't always easy to detect. 2011

~ ~ ~

Thinking is the most conscious activity in our soul. Feeling is dreamlike and Willing is deeply asleep. What matters about thinking is that we have to actively think, and we have to think about thinking. In other words, we have to think about the thoughts that we have. Not all our thoughts are our own. Not all of our thoughts make sense if we really think about them.

The black doves are the thoughts that enter into our mind when it is vacant. These are the moments when we get lazy about our thinking. We get lazy about thinking when we accept other people's ideas instead of thinking something through for ourselves. Or when we don't think something through properly. When we don't actively think, when we don't occupy our thinking - which does take effort - we create vacant spaces in our minds. Simple observation of the world, especially of nature, tells us that voids are always filled by something.

So what fills the void in our minds when our thinking is not active enough? Lucifer and Ahriman enter our brain like parasites and think their thoughts there. This is why we have to close the loft.

Otherwise strange and negative thoughts will occupy our mind - even negative thoughts about those who are close to us.

If we can make room for the Christ force in the temple of our being Christ will cleanse it of all negativity. Then we can love, truly love, our fellow human beings. This means closing the loft on our negative, judgmental, and disagreeing thoughts. Even the simplest negative thought about another person's actions or words damages them.

We can stop these thoughts from even forming and replace them with ideas of understanding and love. For example, if we read something that someone has written that we do not agree with, the purest response is to say to ourselves, "I don't fully understand that, I will remain open to that idea in the hope that I can eventually understand it." That is disciplined thinking, pure and love-filled. 2012

~ ~ ~

We are the temple of Christ. Of all the beings in this Cosmos, we are worthy to be the temple of Christ. The only way we can know him is through our thinking. The only way we can do this is if we understand what thinking actually is. Human beings have only been thinking since about 600BC. Before that we were clairvoyant. We were unconsciously informed by the spiritual worlds.

This ancient clairvoyance is still available to us now, but we must resist it. Through consciously thinking we must come to the new clairvoyance. It is our task to recognise the old black doves and transform them into new and pure white doves. To reach this new clairvoyance we must also resist the pull of modern thinking with its logical concepts dependent on our body and the activity of our nervous system.

Thinking has made a journey from ancient clairvoyance to conceptual thinking, and now we must free it from the nervous system so that it becomes the spiritual capacity of Imagination. The symbol of Spiritual Imagination is the dove. When our I Am is infused with the Cosmic Christ, we have the ability to perceive what lies behind the sense world and see there the outer forms of spirit. This can be confusing and we need a strong connection with our I Am to guide us. We spiritualise our senses by silencing our intellect and we weave mental images in the ether which take on a life of their own. In this way we can know truth if we remain open to it, and if we remain conscious. 2013

~ ~ ~

Why is it so important for us discipline and purify thinking? If we understand what thinking is, as well as why we have the ability to think, we will be able to answer this question. Thinking is the capacity to form mental pictures which we call concepts. We link these concepts or ideas together in the process of thinking so that we can reach conclusions about things.

Of course we know from experience that our conclusions don't always lead us to fully understand things. This tells us that human thinking is an evolving activity. If we understand this much, then we can participate in this evolution in a cooperative way. The real purpose of thinking is to comprehend ourselves as spiritual beings who happen to occupy physical bodies from time to time.

When we comprehend ourselves as spiritual beings we begin to see the value of every human being. This awareness helps us transcend our differences. Out of this experience arises an enormous respect for each other. We see that we each struggle to become aware of our place in the scheme of things. If this is a true experience for us, love wells up for the struggles we each go through. We now go out of our way to avoid adding to each other's burdens.

The third night of the lily becomes an annunciation of the presence of Christ within every human being. We then understand the damage we can do if we think negative thoughts about others. We are filled with the kind of responsibility a mother feels for her unborn infant. Each person in our lives becomes this infant which we can assist to nurture as we all progress along the path to comprehend our true nature. 2014

~ ~ ~

If our goal is to purify ourselves it means we have glimpsed our own impurity. Sometimes we can feel defeated by this lack of purity, when really we should see it as a challenge; a reason to live. All too often when we become aware of our inadequacies we devalue ourselves. We say, "This is me and I fall short, I am not good enough." A dark mood can come over us and we struggle to feel positive. These are the black doves.

When we have this dark experience we have completely missed the point of being able to see our less-than-perfect self. The insight we seek is the exact same insight that enables us to see our imperfections. Seeing these imperfections is no reason to persecute ourselves; seeing them enables us to take a step closer to purification.

"Only the prepared human being who has experienced the hard ordeals, the internal purification, and the catharsis can understand the divine. Hence, the young man is killed who approaches the lily before he is prepared and purified." Rudolf Steiner, Goethe's Secret Revelation. Part II: The Fairy Tale of the Green Snake and the Beautiful Lily.

By accepting our trials and our less-than-perfect characteristics (without excusing them) we change them from negative to positive. Our personal characteristics are like stairs leading up to the lookout where we can see everything in perspective. It is through disciplining our thinking that we accept our individuality, and the individuality of others. If our temple was already pure our life would have no meaning. If we can fully participate in the purification we become co-workers with Christ Jesus. 2015

HOLY NIGHT SIX
December 29-30 - Gemini

The three nights of the sword.

Peter's night. Night of the sword consecration.

Everyone needs to forge by her or himself the sword of discernment. With increased willpower everyone needs forge together (unite) the two pieces; the deathless, the eternal and the ephemeral, to discover the truth.

Mystery: The Son of God, Son of Man merge with Oneness! Rudolf Steiner

6. Heilige Nacht

29./30. – Zwillinge

Die drei Nächte des Schwertes.

Petrus-Nacht. Nacht der Schwertweihe. Jeder muss sich das Schwert der Unterscheidung selbst schmieden. Jeder muss mit gesteigerter Willenskraft die beiden Stücke, das Todlose, Ewige und das Vergängliche zusammenschmieden, um die Wahrheit kennen zu lernen.

Mysterium: Gottessohn mit Menschensohn verschmelzen. Einssein! Rudolf Steiner

Contemplations for the sixth night by Kristina Kaine

Of the three soul forces, the will is the most mysterious. In our lives we deal with two kinds of will; one which is connected to nature and the forces of dissolution and destruction, the other which is connected to spirit and the constructive forces of the earth.

We find the earthly will in our digestive system and other bodily movements – we can't be conscious of it nor interfere with it, it has a job to do. It is the spiritual will that we can wield like a sword. The sword is directed by our moral impulses making us an integral part of the cause and effect that creates this world. We have accepted a great responsibility by taking control of our own will. We were given this responsibility when Christ entered into the earth to give us personal possession of our I Am.

So what is morality? It is greatly misrepresented and has little to do with what we do, but rather how we do it. Our activity can only be moral when our happiness is not acquired at the expense of others. So if we are happy to have a new iPad which was made in a factory where the workers are badly treated, or we are happy to buy the cheapest food produced by animals that are badly treated and so on, we are caught up in a web of immorality. Acts of morality arise when our deeds originate from our interest in other people. Morality arises out of love, the purest, highest love and respect for others. 2011

~ ~ ~

Peter is the disciple who struck the high priest's slave and cut off his right ear. Then Jesus told him off for interfering with his journey to the cross. After that Peter lied about knowing Jesus. How many times do we do this today in our own lives? We long to be able to act in the right way in every situation but sometimes it doesn't work out that way. Does this matter? Isn't it here that we actually become aware of our will? We experience our will in our action and then again in our regret. Then we can exercise our will to settle ourselves down so that we are not consumed by what happened.

It follows that if we never did anything wrong we wouldn't be aware of our will. Part of our process of becoming the Son of Man, of giving birth to our Self, our full humanity, is to use our will with awareness. Engaging with this process as consciously as possible is our present task.

It can be daunting to think of doing this work and we might be inclined to put it off. However, if we can just observe our will, even in the smallest things, an awakening will take place. The main difficulty comes when we try to do it only from an earthly perspective. We cannot know truth with our earthly mind because the very nature of our earthly mind means that we have forgotten truth. Truth, aletheia, means overcoming forgetting. We will only be able to overcome our forgetting when Christ fills our I Am and the Son of Man unites with the Son of God within us. Only then will we have the strength to see the truth, to unforget. It all begins with the small moments of becoming aware of the way we use our sword, our will. 2012

~ ~ ~

To consecrate the sword means to hold sacred our human will. Of all the beings in the universe, we have the sacred and holy privilege of using our will at our own discretion. Would we pick up a sword in defence if we were not familiar with the sword? To do so could mean that we cut ourselves, or that the sword is used against us.

What is this will? We unfold the impulse of our will in our action and activity. We are not aware of it until we see the results of the action. We will not be fully aware of our will until we can consecrate it - this is a safety mechanism. To consecrate our will means that we set it apart, make it holy, dedicate it to activity that is eternal, immortal and imperishable - true! When we do this we become the Son of Man and the whole of humanity are our brothers and sisters. Then we will not use our will in a way that disadvantages another person.

Our will is very individual; we can think the same thoughts, we can come together to share a feeling but it is rare that two people can act in the same way at once (unrehearsed). Wielding a sword is a very individual activity. 2013

~ ~ ~

How do we experience the eternal and the immortal? This is difficult in a world focussing on the present and valuing instant gratification. It is not easy to understand concepts like eternal and immortal unless we understand that we live repeated lives on this earth; and not just in theory but to have the ability to apply ideas about reincarnation in our daily life.

If, for example, we clash with someone and our first response is to wonder about our relationship with them in a past life, we immediately get in touch with the eternal. We are able to stand in the present and consider the past, and decide to take action which will influence the future.

In a similar way we experience the immortal and the perishable. It requires that we stand in our I AM. This sword is our I AM resting in the sheath of our body. We forged our sword in previous lives and continue to forge it in this life. Our job is to learn how to wield it, but first we must become aware of it. To wield a sword blindly can cause quite a bit of damage.

We begin by placing our hands on the hilt of the sword while we work on purifying our will. This work means that we become much more aware of our motives. Gradually, over time, as we become more observant of our interactions with others we become more able to respond objectively. If someone is mean to us and we remain calm inside, in this way we are responding in an eternal way. Then we resolve our karma; the consequences of our actions in a past life. We do this by recognizing the truth of the situation and we consciously set ourselves free from the bond by unifying past and present. Then we can walk into the future with increased freedom. 2014

~ ~ ~

When we contemplate the deathless, the eternal, comparing it with the ephemeral, the temporary, at some point we meet the idea of reincarnation. That is, unless we think of eternity as a void.

Through the idea of reincarnation we begin to accept that this temporary state we call earthly life is part of a continual stream of existence; like a dolphin dipping in and out of the water. We existed before we were born and we exist after we die, albeit in a different state of being. None of these states is any less real than the other.

If we accept this, we can begin to imagine what it is like to exist without a physical body. As a spiritual being do we have a consciousness like this one, or do we float around nebulously merged with Universe? The answer to this question is directly linked to the level of conscious awareness we achieve during our incarnation. The level of consciousness we achieve in any particular life is a direct result of the way in which we use our will, our sword. This in turn is a measure of our ability to become the Son of Man, the self-born.

As we explore these ideas we can turn our attention to the kind of person we were in previous lives. Were we male or female or were we able to merge these two expressions to some extent. Were we emotional or intellectual or a combination of the two. In this way we can begin to awaken memories of past lives. There are no set rules for each of us is different.

One experience which can be helpful in daily life is to observe the way others treat us or the way we treat them. This is usually a mirror of the way we treated them in a past life. If they respect us, we respected them. If they bully us, we may have bullied them. Regardless, it is important to meet the other person with openness and love, - which can require a lot of will power in some cases as we know. Our aim is not to eradicate karma from our life, karma is a crucial part of our development. We should also be mindful that sometimes our interactions with others is setting up a karmic relationship for a future life enabling us to take a large step towards oneness - uniting the two-edged sword. 2015

HOLY NIGHT SEVEN
December 30-31 - Cancer

The serpent in the hilt of the sword: wisdom. Occupy yourselves with elevated lectures. It is the night of the great commandment.

The mystery of activity: Who orders our soul? Who is the Lord of our soul, the author of our actions? We have the freedom to strengthen the good will in us. Rudolf Steiner

7. Heilige Nacht

30./31. – Krebs

Die Schlange am Schwertknauf: Weisheit. Man soll sich mit erhebender Lektüre beschäftigen. Es ist die Nacht des großen Befehles.

Das Mysterium der Tätigkeit: Wer befiehlt über unsere Seele? Wer ist der Herr unserer Seele, der Täter unserer Taten? Wir haben die Freiheit, den guten Willen in uns zu stärken. Rudolf Steiner

Contemplations for the seventh night by Kristina Kaine

As we become more aware of our three soul forces, our feeling or sentience, our thoughts or intellect and our will or conscious awareness, we see many repetitive patterns. We realise that we are inclined to have certain feelings, think certain thoughts and behave in a certain way. Everyone who knows us can tell us about this. Profilers study it and can predict how we respond to particular situations. This is our personality and our character. These personal inclinations have developed lifetime after lifetime. The strength of our character and the disposition of our personality can be directly related to the influence of our I Am in our soul.

It is our I Am that thinks in our soul, it is our I Am that arouses certain feelings in our soul, and it is our I Am that motivates us to behave in particular ways. If we allow this to happen unconsciously then we are no more than a puppet. We have no freedom and no understanding of the events in our life. What is more, under some circumstances we can react unfavourably.

Every single thing that happens to us is caused by something we ourselves did in a past life. Now we meet the effect of what we caused. This could appear to be quite destructive however it is quite the opposite. Everything we have done was for the express purpose of becoming aware of our I Am. Our path is one of pain and sorrow as played out in the life of Jesus the Christened One. We follow in his footsteps for he is that great I Am who walked this earth in completeness. He shows us the way. It is our choice how we meet the consequences of our own actions; we can suffer in pain or we can experience the joy that comes with being aware that we are fulfilling our purpose. 2011

~ ~ ~

The great commandment is written in St John's Gospel: "A new commandment I give to you, that you love one another; even as I have loved you, that you also love one another." Jn 13:34

Wisdom is something that has developed over aeons; it is part of the fibre of our being. Through this wisdom this earth and our human being-ness was created. We are not fully aware of this wisdom, we seek it continually. We could say that our quest for wisdom motivates us to live on this earth. We can only understand wisdom, and apply it, through our I Am. So we could say that wisdom and our I Am go hand in hand through life; as we become aware of one so we also begin to use the other.

These concepts are discussed in Rudolf Steiner's "An Outline of Esoteric Science" Chapter 6. "Wisdom is the prerequisite for love; love is the result of wisdom that has been reborn in the "I" p 397 It is up to us to express love. Even to love when love is not returned.

We should also always ask ourselves the question: Who is the master of our soul? In every situation in life, who rules our soul? All too often it is the serpent, that original ego that has served us so well. Now we must guide the serpent into the hilt so that it is under our control. In this way we work consciously with our I Am and we experience true freedom. To be able to really love someone with whom we have difficult karma is true freedom. Good will arises in the harmonious existence of two opposites. This would suggest that we need the two opposites so that we can introduce the harmony. The work is in the act of creating harmony which is our free choice; this is our good will at work. 2012

~ ~ ~

Is there a person on this earth who is not familiar with the image of the serpent in the Garden of Eden? It is important to understand the esoteric truth behind this image. Then we will understand the true nature of love and the Great Commandment that we should love one another from John 13:34

When we truly love another person, they will love us in return and then we both experience pure love that contains no self-interest. When our love is biased, motivated by our own needs, the serpent is always involved. The serpent is Lucifer. In the Garden of Eden, it was his job to lure human souls to enter into physical bodies and participate in this material world. At that time, we were androgynous spirits and the entry into the physical world meant that we split into male and female. The purpose for this was so that humans could produce a physical body so pure that the Cosmic Christ could enter into it and in this way give every human being the freedom to become self-realised individuals and eventually become gods themselves.

We can only begin to do this when we rule in our own souls. Each one of us has this responsibility. As we connect with our I Am, as we become consciously aware of feeling, thinking, and will, we wield our own sword. In this way we also redeem Lucifer, whose task is done, and we strengthen the good will in us. 2013

~ ~ ~

How well do we understand freedom? We want to be free but how can we be free? Freedom is not given to us, freedom is ours if we create it. One of the main purposes for incarnating on the earth is to become free. To the extent to which we claim our freedom here on earth is the extent to which we can have freedom in the spiritual worlds between incarnations. If we can understand this and work towards it we will also have wisdom.

As beings of body, soul and spirit we should understand that freedom is a spiritual activity. In our body we cannot be free because we are not yet wise enough to guide the physical activity of our body that keeps us alive and incarnated. For the most part our soul leans towards our physical existence, but if we allow our spirit more influence in our soul we will experience the truth about freedom.

So how do we gain freedom? Primarily though self awareness. It is through our level of self awareness that we can control our prejudices, bringing balance and understanding to our sympathies and antipathies. To like one thing and dislike another is a lower instinct; we cannot experience freedom if we are biased. True freedom comes when we find something to like about something we dislike.

In essence, freedom happens when we infuse our thinking with will. Love, the great commandment, happens when we infuse our will with thoughts. 2014

~ ~ ~

Occupying ourselves with spiritual truth is an important task, now more so than ever before. Esoteric knowledge has been a carefully guarded secret for so long and has only been freely available in the last century or so. Even though we have access to so much esoteric information today, this does not mean it is easy to understand. We also have to deal with the misinterpretation of this knowledge. This is why it is so important to occupy ourselves with it. The word occupy means to take possession of, to seize it, to grasp it and make it part of us.

It is of great benefit to our soul if we set aside time to read elevated lectures, even for 10 minutes, and then with strengthened will consider what we have read. In this way we reawaken spiritual knowledge that has remained hidden from today's consciousness. The Lord of our soul, our I Am, has access to all knowledge. When we begin to connect with our I Am we gain access to this knowledge. We also come to understand that our access to spiritual knowledge is on a need to know basis. In fact, sometimes we forget what we know until there is a reason for it to come to mind.

The other important thing to understand is that esoteric knowledge must be applied in a practical way in our life. Once we have taken possession of it we can't cast it aside and revert to our old way of thinking. It can be challenging to respond to life's situation with spiritual understanding. It is up to us to work out how we can do this. Once a spiritual truth reveals itself to us, it must become part of the way we think, feel and act. We can't say we understand love and then not love someone who annoyed us. Nor can we pretend to love them, it must be genuine. In this way we exercise our freedom to strengthen our good will. 2015

HOLY NIGHT EIGHT
December 31 - January 1 - Leo

The cross on the pommel (the counterweight at the end of the hilt): Sacrifice. The tongue, girded with the sword of Christ Power, speaks the truth without being able to hurt. It is the night of horror.

Mystery: The knight, the fighter with the lance of the will and the sword of knowledge. The dog as a symbol of obedience, by his side. Behind him, death and the devil! On certain levels of knowledge, each false step leads rapidly to destruction, the victory will be achieved through the fulfillment and the unremitting faithfulness to the duties of the lion. Rudolf Steiner

8. Heilige Nacht
31./1. – Löwe

Das Kreuz am Schwertknauf: Das Opfer. Umgürtet mit dem Schwert der Christuskraft spricht die Zunge die Wahrheit, ohne verletzen zu können. Es ist die Nacht des Entsetzens.

Mysterium: Der Ritter, der Streiter mit der Lanze des Willens und dem Schwert der Erkenntnis. Der Hund als Symbol des Gehorsams, ihm zur Seite. Hinter ihm Tod und Teufel! Auf bestimmter Erkenntnisstufe führt jeder falsche Schritt schneller ins Verderben, der Sieg wird errungen durch das Erfülltsein und der unermüdlichen Treue gegenüber den Aufgaben des Löwen. Rudolf Steiner

Contemplations for the eighth night by Kristina Kaine

On the eighth Holy Night we stand on the precipice between two rounds of time; 2011 and 2012. There has to be a crucifixion. All that has served our growth during the past year must now be crucified, it must die. Imagine the consequences if Jesus had not been crucified … .

All our precious thoughts, feelings and actions that have brought us this far can be put to rest. As we step over the threshold into the New Year we can raise them to a new level. When we sacrifice all that is precious in our soul, that served us throughout the year, we can put it to service for others. The depth of feeling that we experienced for spiritual truth can become compassion for the misfortune of others. Not just, "I'm sorry" but a real experience of the crushing sorrow that is felt by them.

The new thoughts that we were able to think in our soul because we understood some spiritual truth now paves the way for living Inspiration in our spirit. Even though that spiritual truth was like gold for us we must loosen our grip on it. We can never possess spiritual truth, it belongs to the universe. If we let it go it will come back to us when we need it, if we hang onto it we may not be able to find it when we need it.

The new actions that we were proud to put in place during the year must also be crucified. To hang onto them proudly is egotistical. Through our will we reveal who we really are; we allow others to know us and we can know them. To try to know others without revealing anything of ourselves is destructive for all concerned.

As we take this next step we are reassured by the presence of Christ Jesus who took it before us. 2011 - 2012

~ ~ ~

What ideas do we have about the presence of Christ within us? Is he a light, is he a healer, is he a protector? How often do we see him crucified within us? Are we prepared to experience this crucifixion or do we put it off, or worse, say that it won't happen within us?

Every detail of the life of Jesus the Christened One will take place in our being. The very point of recording it in sacred scripture is to prepare us for the experience. It is nonsense to think that Jesus experienced it for us. He paved the way so that we could actually experience it ourselves.

In the image of the crucifixion painted by Giuliano di Simone we can identify all the kinds of activity in our body, soul and spirit. There is purity and there is violence, action and lack of action, understanding and lack of understanding and so on. At the core of all of this is fear and horror if we dare to look. We cannot deny that a crucifixion is horrific.

Can we accept that fear and horror are part of life? It is through fear that we become aware of ourselves. It is through overcoming fear that we become aware of our I AM. Victory comes when we know our inner Christ as he really is. 2012-13

~ ~ ~

This is the third night of the sword. The imagery in these words point to the crucifixion. It was the spear that allowed the blood of Jesus to pour out into the earth and complete the task for which he came. His task was to make this earth the body of Christ restoring its dwindling life-force. Without this earth, human beings cannot develop their full potential.

We can only achieve our full potential through the purest will. Our task to become aware of our will so that we use it responsibly. Each time we misuse our will we are working with death and the devil and we create new karma. At a certain level, the misuse of our will must be taken care of by the Lord of Karma, who is Christ, to prevent Cosmic consequences.

This night, at the turning point between two years, is a time for weighing up the past and stepping into the future with purpose. It is a time to have the courage to say that we do not know the truth, that we only have glimpses of it. It is a time to assess the level of respect that we have for the Christ deed. It is also a time to commit ourselves to becoming more aware of how we use our will. Even at the simplest level in our opinions and judgments of others. We cannot know people's karma and therefore we cannot know why they have their particular character and personality. At this level of the will, we can at least give people the space to be themselves, and then we will hold the sword of power that cannot hurt. 2013-14

~ ~ ~

Why are we often fearful of making a wrong move? Perhaps because we know that the slightest mistake will usually bring some form of criticism - self criticism or criticism from others. Perhaps this is a good thing because it prepares us for that time when we reach a certain level of knowledge and mistakes can have serious consequences. However, we should not be paralysed by fear. We have to gain esoteric insight, that is our personal responsibility, and it is the reason we have incarnated into the flesh. Our commitment to our spiritual development can only be one hundred percent, there can be no half measures.

As we stand on the cusp of 2015 we can make a promise to ourselves to take our spiritual understanding to a new level. The thing about spiritual knowledge is that if our commitment is genuine the knowledge opens up to us. If not, then spiritual truth will make no sense to us. Perhaps this is why this is the night of fear and horror; a window opens and we review the results of our efforts over the past year and then we see how the new year will pan out if we don't make a new resolve.

We must become like the knight who has sharpened his will, gained knowledge and is accompanied by obedience. He leaves his meeting with death and the devil behind.

Our victory depends on our ability to see that we are actually divine beings. Of all the beings in the Cosmos we are the ones able to take into ourselves the presence of the mighty Cosmic Christ who entered the body of Jesus and became human (briefly). Why did he do this? So that we could claim our freedom and overcome karma. If we continue to act out of our karma and only engage with others through their karma, 2015 will be much tougher than it should be - not only for us but for the world. Let's not drag death and the devil with us; they will express themselves through us, through our dead consciousness, by stirring up our karma. We can only avoid this by nurturing our relationship with Christ knowing that through him we can have ALL knowledge. 2014-15

~ ~ ~

Spiritual development has consequences. As we develop our ability to see truth, the first thing we see is the truth about our own nature, especially our lower nature. Are we strong enough to deal with this? Can we counterbalance our higher and lower nature? It is for this reason that we need a relationship with Christ. He will help us see the flaws of our lower nature and deal with the horror we feel. We must always remember that our life is not just about facing difficulties; the difficulties are there giving us something to overcome and in this way hone our will.

When the Christ Power speaks we are reminded that it is the Logos, the Creative Word, resounding through the universe from the beginning of creation. Of course we won't measure up to the perfection of the Creative Word, nor will we be hurt by it. Knowing about these experiences prepares us by strengthening us and helping us to realise that without the lower self we would never be in a position to have a personal experience of ourselves as eternal beings.

This is a tricky time in our development. Even if we are unsure of the Christ Being - which is understandable because he has been so misunderstood and misrepresented - we can decide to develop some confidence in his purity and power. Simply through our openness and willingness to meet Christ, we leave death and the anti-forces behind. Leaving them behind doesn't mean they disappear, we simply see them for what they are - stages on our journey.

While these ideas may seem daunting, we can be sure that we each have deep levels of courage (lion) to face any danger. We also have companions on our journey who lovingly support our efforts. 2015-16.

HOLY NIGHT NINE
January 1-2 - Virgo

Now follow the three nights of the crown.

Detachment from intellect alone, or separate the intellect from the earthly bondage and purposefulness. It is the Triple Holy Night in which the lower self surrenders and there remains only the desire to serve, to give oneself. Rudolf Steiner

9. Heilige Nacht

1./2. – Jungfrau

Nun folgen die drei Nächte der Krone.

Loslösung vom Nur-Intellekt oder die Loslösung des Intellektes von der irdischen Gebundenheit und Zweckhaftigkeit. Es ist die dreimal heilige Nacht, in der das niedere Ich abfällt und nur der Wunsch bleibt, zu dienen, sich hinzugeben. Rudolf Steiner

Contemplations for the ninth night by Kristina Kaine

Our personal resurrection is accompanied by a new level of objectivity. We won't take things as personally as we did before. This doesn't mean that we will meet every event in our lives with equanimity, but we will find a greater level of detachment than we have in past.

Whenever we can be detached we know that we are responding to life through our I Am. Otherwise, we respond with our lower self which behaves like a child in some situations. It wants its own way, which is usually the way of least resistance. Yet if we do resist responding as we usually do to something that annoys us we feel liberated. Try it. The next time someone annoys you take a breath, create a space and say to yourself, "If this was happening to someone else would I be annoyed?"

In this way we activate our will to control our lower emotional responses. We let the words or actions of the other person wash over us and flow away into oblivion. When we do this whatever they did loses its intensity and everyone benefits.

Furthermore, if we remember that we attract whatever happens to us then we could quickly recognize these little tests and see them as a way of strengthening our New Year resolves. 2012

~ ~ ~

What are these three crowns? A crown signifies rulership. When we have inner rulership we could earn a crown for each of the three areas over which we have dominion.

The first area to be controlled is our emotions and feelings. We instinctively express our feelings through our lower self. In this state we are focused on our own welfare. We play our own tune; we sound our own individual note often not harmonizing with the notes played by all those around us. Or we don't play our note at all because the notes played by others drown us out.

If we can detach our intellect from its earthly and practical cares we release our Imagination. This Imagination is a spiritual faculty of immense significance. This is the point at which we rise above our soul and begin to express ourselves through our spirit. We experience the wisdom of universal order. We begin to see the living universal archetypes. We realize how our own self-interest could affect the true order of things.

Now we begin to feel the crown on our head and the responsibility of the embryonic child that is our I AM. Our self-serving feelings become ennobled revealing to us spiritual Imaginations of our true Self. Antisocial feelings and abstract thinking dissolve into living images that assist us to understand the world order. This assuredness has a stabilizing influence on us and we are able to integrate ourselves more easily into the true flow of life. 2013

~ ~ ~

The crowns can represent our spiritual faculties of Imagination, Inspiration and Intuition. It is our goal to earn these crowns. Even though these faculties will not be fully developed in us for quite some time, they do begin to emerge now in preparation. If we don't prepare ourselves for the emergence of these faculties, mental difficulties can arise. This could be one explanation for the rising mental instability we see today in the population.

The first crown is that of Imagination. When we free our intellect from its physical expression, thoughts arise that have no physical cause. We actually begin to tap into cosmic thoughts, the source of thoughts. When we see these pure thoughts we understand that our true purpose is to become consciously aware of the mystery of the cosmos and participate in it fully.

To achieve this level of awareness, we need to know that in our soul, thinking, feeling and will are integrated. To achieve spiritual consciousness, we need to learn to separate them and reunite them at will. Some situations require a lot of thinking and only a little bit of feeling, other situations require a lot of will with just a bit a feeling. We can practice doing this with annoying issues that arise in daily life. If we don't learn to do it, and our thinking separates, and feeling and will are not added according to the demands of a situation, we can go insane. If we foster our relationship with Christ, he will guide us through this process, he went through it himself with the Crowning with Thorns. 2014

~ ~ ~

To be able to wear the crown indicates we have some control over our soul's responses to life. This control comes from our ability to be objective. The one thing that works against us as we try to be objective is our karma.

Our earthly and practical cares arise from the particular karma we chose to work on in this life. The people we meet in life are the ones who can assist us to make the necessary karmic adjustments. That is their job if you like. These adjustments can only be achieved through detachment. Unless we think this through we will never understand why we face difficulties in our lives and we will usually seek to blame the other person.

Once we work it out, which usually means that we have committed to a path of spiritual development, we begin to wear the crown. Then we should ask the question: Do we place the crown on our heads because of the value we place on ourselves? Or have we earned the crown because our lower self surrenders?

One of the difficulties arising on the spiritual path to truth is to overvalue ourselves; we separate ourselves from the life we were leading and we can think of ourselves as self-crowned Holy people. As a result we are more egotistical than ever. This is why we must work on our desire to serve and to be integrated with the world around us.

Separating ourselves, and thinking that we are better than others, is not the path to the future. Our role model Jesus was constantly criticized for mixing with the wrong people. When we wear the invisible crown we have earned, and go about our daily business, we quietly set an example to all those we come into contact with. When they notice that we are different, they are changed. It is an unspoken blessing that pours from our heart to theirs. 2015

~ ~ ~

Intellect is everything connected with forming concepts and mental pictures. As a stand-alone activity it can be quite lifeless and quite isolating. When we read spiritual information trying to make sense of it we can become trapped in our intellect and may be inclined to draw diagrams and make dot points. This is fine in the beginning but unless we progress from there, then all we have is second-hand information, we haven't made it our own. We can only wear the crown when we have experienced truth firsthand. We do this by infusing our thinking with will.

Thinking is an etheric activity and our goal is to make it as pure as possible. We arrive at pure thinking when our thoughts are not stimulated by an external object, our thinking is then sense-free which makes it selfless. This is why our lower self surrenders and we have the desire to serve.

What do we serve? We serve the purpose of creation. As each of us manages to experience pure thinking, we contribute in a selfless way to evolution. Our ego steps out of the way, no longer a disruption to self and others.

Therefore in our reading, in our contemplation and in the way we apply what we have read to the way we live our life, we align ourselves with the earth's purpose. We let go of our habitual responses to life and we remain open to new ways of being, new ways of seeing and we find new ways to contribute. This selflessness is not altruistic, it does not sacrifice self for others, we stand in community with others working for the greater good in every possible way. 2016.

10 HOLY NIGHT TEN
January 2-3 - Libra

The night in which the highest offering of service increases; obedience-listening-hearing to learn, to the inner voice and the signs of the Divine.

Mystery: The voice in us through various incarnations: Its clarity increases by sacrifice and decision. Rudolf Steiner

> 10. Heilige Nacht
>
> 2./3. Januar – Waage

Die Nacht, in der aus dem Dienen das größte Opfer erwächst, Gehorsam-Horchen-Hören lernen, auf die innere Stimme und das Zeichen des Göttlichen.

Mysterium: Der Rufer in uns durch die verschiedenen Inkarnationen hindurch: Seine Klarheit nimmt zu durch Opfer und Entscheidung. Rudolf Steiner

Contemplations for the tenth night by Kristina Kaine

Do we hear our I Am calling to us? Do we strive to experience this I Am in our being, in our soul? Do we try to remember the agreement that we made with it before we incarnated? If we do we will be undisturbed by success and failure, good and evil, joy and suffering for we will see that these are important experiences necessary for our development.

Our I Am directs us to resolve our karma, to create harmony with all the people in our lives. Of course we would rather keep away from some people in our lives, thinking that then our lives will be more enjoyable. We do not remove our difficulties in this way; they will be re-presented to us through other people. If we are honest with ourselves we will admit that it is easier to hate those who make our lives difficult rather than to love them. Hate is considered to be a strong word, but the fact is, the polar opposite of love is hate. It is better to face the truth of this word than to gloss over it and give it a nicer name.

If we know anything at all about our I Am we realise that we are challenged to serve every single person in our life, not one single person is in our life by accident. The way we serve all those who are gathered around us is to love them, truly love them. Every human being is sacred, every human being has the potential to become a god. Do we want to be in the company of something that is sacred? something that is becoming a god? 2012

~ ~ ~

How well do we understand the concept of sacrifice? Very often our sacrifice has a hidden selfish motivate. For some reason we don't understand that if we give and give this gesture will be returned to us. The giving however must not be motivated by what we will get. True sacrifice is motivated by love.

Angels love. Their whole existence is sacrifice which is dedicated to us so that we may become fully human. "For the creation waits with eager longing for the revealing of the sons of God;" Rm 8:19

Angels also speak to us. We can only hear their voices when we are able to use our faculty of spiritual Inspiration. This inner hearing comes as a response to our commitment to understand our full potential.

This inner hearing takes place when we engage with our I Am and think outside our body. Our thinking no longer needs our brain, it also no longer relies on remembered concepts; this thinking has access to universal thought. In this way we place the second crown on our heads. We begin to understand that life after life we have worked towards this goal.

Now, finally we hear the words we have longed to hear, the words of Christ. They resound within us as a personal conversation; "Peace be with you" to remove any alarm in our soul. "Love one another as I have loved you" as a new Commandment when we are not sure what to do. "I am with you even to the end of this age" when we are fearful and anxious. In this way we are assisted to make the decision. 2013

~ ~ ~

The second night of the crown speaks to us of the spiritual faculty of Inspiration. This is not the primitive consciousness of premonition but rather hearing a clear inner voice speaking to us. When we hear this voice, we know what is true and what is not true. We experience Inspiration when feeling is freed from our body. The feelings that we usually experience are mirrored reflections of cosmic Inspiration, they are not the real thing.

As the word Inspiration suggests, it is connected with the breath and the rhythms of the heart and lungs. We know that we take our first breath when we leave the womb and take possession of our incarnation as a human being. There is a connection here between this life and our previous lives that lie behind us. When we experience Inspiration, we begin to discover our own pre-earthly existence, especially as it relates to this incarnation.

Sacrifice and service are connected with this because we cannot enter into these great mysteries unless we are fully prepared. We must come to the point of fully understanding what it means to serve. What are we serving? We are serving the cosmos and its creators. They are waiting for us to come to this knowledge. They have served us; by giving us life and the freedom to use this life as we choose. Now we must strive to understand how we can serve them and how this is connected with sacrifice. We find the clues when we look at the life of Jesus; his birth, and his role in the baptism, crucifixion, and resurrection. This is what helps us make the decision. 2014

~ ~ ~

The second night of the crown focuses on service and sacrifice. We could say that the first crown is earned when we use our feeling-will, by integrating our will into our feeling. This second crown is more to do with infusing our thinking with will. This means that we become aware of our thoughts, we control our thoughts and we make sure that we think actively rather than letting random thoughts flow through our mind. Then, when we are required to concentrate and think carefully, our will-filled thinking can bring about the best result. How many times in a day do we realize that we didn't think; we didn't take into account all the factors before we acted?

When we begin to consciously think, we place ourselves in service to the Cosmos. The word 'serve' in Greek is diakoneo which literally means "kicking up dust." Through our thinking we disturb this settled earth. We begin to see signs of the divine plan in us. We send a signal that we are willing to understand why the Universe has been created in the way it has. We also realise that it has been specifically created this way to serve us. Every tree provides us with the oxygen necessary for life, and every mineral, plant and animal works to nourish us. We begin to take into account the beings of the Spiritual Hierarchy who work to keep everything in balance so that we can integrate our I Am into our being. How often do we take all this for granted? How do we feel when our hard work is not acknowledged?

Service and sacrifice go hand in hand. The word 'sacrifice' in Greek is thusia, which means "the act of offering." It describes the way in which we offer up our worldly, self-centred will for universal good. This doesn't mean we sacrifice our own position, we add to the universal effort thereby adding to ourselves. In service and sacrifice we become the co-creators and the second crown is placed on our heads. 2015

~ ~ ~

Do we hear to learn or do we hear to satisfy our ego? We can test this by thinking about how we feel when someone pays us a complement or criticises us. This Holy Night is the time to observe our inner reactions; they are noisy and can obscure the sweet, soft inner voice telling us that we are immortal and we are Divine. We are the beings chosen to carry the I Am through many cycles of life on this earth and life in the spiritual worlds.

Obedience is about accepting our responsibility to hear the inner voice, the voice that speaks of the true nature of our being that continually incarnates. The clarity of the voice depends on our ability to achieve inner stillness. The commitment to hear this voice is a decision we make to become aware of who we really are. This also comes with our decision to make a contribution to evolution. Each time we watch the news and find ourselves criticizing the behaviour of others, we soon realize that their consciousness is the result of our own contribution to human life in our past lives.

If the full truth of this hits home we can be consumed with a sense of shame, or we can take a decision to make a difference for the future incarnations of humanity. This is when we increase our highest offering of service. We each do this in our own way, in our own environment, always honouring each other's task to be the best we can be. We can be our best when we sacrifice our reactions, always observing, and always looking for new ways to hear the inner voice. 2016

HOLY NIGHT ELEVEN
January 3-4 - Libra

The eleventh night: The struggle with the Guardian of the Threshold.

Mystery: The Grail builds up in us. To always increase our allegiance to the Highest! Rudolf Steiner

11. Heilige Nacht

3./4. Januar - Skorpion

Die elfte Nacht: Der Kampf mit dem Hüter der Schwelle.

Mysterium: Die Gralsburg in uns aufbauen. Sich immer mehr in Treue zum höchsten bekennen! Rudolf Steiner

Contemplations for the eleventh night by Kristina Kaine

Humanity lives on the threshold of the spiritual world. Some say that we have passed over it unconsciously. This means that we wield spiritual power without knowing it. Therefore there is an urgent call for human beings to become consciously aware that they are spiritual beings. We can only do this if we realise that our spiritual I-being is animating us, using us just as we use any instrument in this physical world. Just as we pick up a spoon and place food in our mouth, our I Am is placing us in situations with other people that will be food for its development.

When we get this, when we actually think the thoughts associated with this in the moments in our life when our karma is being played out, we have an I Am experience. We are in touch with who we really are and we observe what is before us with interest just as we would observe our dinner plate with interest. We can see all that we like and all that we dislike without bias.

This is when, through our own striving, we receive into ourselves the power of the blood of Christ, the Holy Grail. Our blood is the vehicle of our I Am and when we purify our blood of its lower desires and instincts we make it a fitting substance for our own I Am, then our blood becomes purer still so that it can become the blood of Christ. Are we up to the task? 2012

~ ~ ~

Can we accept that Christ is a living force that is transforming our blood into his blood? What then is the difference between our blood and his blood? Blood is the physical expression of our I Am. It is our inner fire. As we know, fire can be both useful and harmful. Then we might ask how blood can be useful or harmful.

Through our blood we are connected to our family, our race and our nation. It was through the purification of the Jewish bloodline that Jesus could be born and become the first human to carry the Christ force within his body. Imagine the effect that this had on his blood. Then, on the cross, this blood poured out of him. He didn't keep it confined to his race and his elite group. He poured it out and made it available to everyone. While blood is confined to a group we will be at war; when blood is shared freely we will be united through peace.

This means that we loosen our grip on our physical body and live more frequently in our etheric body. Our etheric body becomes lighter, more vibrant and spiritualised and our physical substance becomes less dense. In this way the Holy Grail is formed within our being; our blood becomes Christened. This is when we meet the Guardian of Threshold who tests us to see if we are ready to manage this transformation. How does he test us? By observing how well we combine our feeling, thinking and will as we look at the detail of all our past lives. We have to be able to bear this if we are to progress spiritually. We can only bear it if we experience the presence of the resurrected Christ flowing through our veins. 2013

~ ~ ~

The third crown is the crown of Intuition. Through the faculty of Intuition we live in the reality of the spiritual worlds. Our will is freed from our body. We experience Intuition when we live in our I Am. To do this we quieten the pull of all that is earthly in us. Yet, at the same time, we remain rooted in this earth and in our incarnation. Our ability to do this is the Holy Grail.

We have built the finest Grail Castle by purifying our thinking, feeling, and will. Out of this purified soul, our I Am comes into expression and our spiritual faculties come to life. While we won't be able to do this fully for quite some time, we can experience it from time to time now. The Holy Nights is one of the times when we have the greatest opportunity to do this.

The work that we do in our soul, and the experience we have of our I Am, gives us the strength to meet the Guardian of the Threshold. This Guardian is a supersensible being whom we have brought into existence through our own feelings, thoughts, and actions. Now nothing is hidden from us. The Guardian reveals to us how, through our karma, we have a particular character and specific inclinations. Through the Guardian we understand why we have had to experience all the events in our lives.

In these moments, we can experience the wisdom and love of the cosmos as it guides us to participate in restoring the harmony that is jeopardised by the activity of our own soul. 2014

~ ~ ~

The third crown reveals our pure will - we could call it will-filled will. It means that we are infusing our earthly will with spiritual will. Will is a directive force, in its purest form is creates. It is this will which we need if we are to meet the Guardian of the Threshold and survive the struggle that comes with this meeting. Who is this Guardian? It is our True Self, the highest expression of our I Am. If we think we don't like aspects of our personality now, when we meet our True Self we will see all these aspects in full reality. It could be that the things we dislike in ourselves are actually our strengths, and vice versa.

It is the Guardian's role to prevent us from entering the spiritual worlds prematurely. Our life is a preparation for this crossing. The best preparation we can undertake is to work as consciously as possible with feeling, thinking and willing. Not only that, but also to stop being biased by what we like and dislike. Then we stop being critical of others, we allow them to be themselves as we also accept ourselves as we are. This is what is meant by purifying our will; it is a mighty tool which gives us infinite control over ourselves.

At this stage in human evolution it is critical that we work with our will, imposing it on ourselves not others. While this seems challenging, we are assisted by the inner Grail Forces. We receive these Grail Forces as our blood becomes the blood of Christ. The sign that this is happening is when we "leave everything ... house, brothers, sisters, mothers, fathers, children and lands for my sake" (roughly translated words spoken by Jesus recorded in Mt 19:29-30). Not that we will actually leave them but the Christ force in our being takes precedent. How do we know that this is happening? When we love, truly love, one another. We see the beauty in everyone we meet because we see Christ in them before we see any of their perceived faults. Then we wear the third crown. 2015

~ ~ ~

Do we see ourselves as beings of soul and spirit using our body to dwell on this earth? If we pause for a moment to imagine this, we can become aware that there are no boundaries for our soul and spirit except those we ourselves impose. Boundaries are imposed when we focus on our corporeality.

These boundaries are however necessary to contain our personal striving for freedom. As we achieve freedom here and there, it is the Guardian of the Threshold who, like a thermometer, ensures that this striving contains the right amount of warmth.

Alongside the goal of perfection we will always fall short; achieving perfection is a process. What matters most is that we always increase our allegiance to the Highest. Only through our inner soul work will we discover the path that leads to the Holy Grail. Rudolf Steiner says, "This is a task of cognition, this is a social task. It is also a task that, to the greatest extent possible, is hated in the present." 17 April, 1921

The only way to stop hating this task is to love our life and all the opportunities it offers. Every annoyance is an opportunity to overcome being annoyed. On the other hand, whenever we feel indifferent towards something we have an opportunity to generate interest. These are the ways we regulate the temperature in soul and align ourselves with the Highest. Imagine if the Hierarchy who holds this Universe in balance allowed annoyance and indifference to influence their task.

It is only though inner striving combined with an increase to our allegiance to the Highest that we receive into ourselves the power of the blood of Christ, the Holy Grail. 2016

HOLY NIGHT TWELVE
January 4-5 - Sagittarius

In the Twelfth night- place the crown we have won at the feet of the Divine because we have indeed struggled ourselves, however, that we could achieve it is grace, is the spiritual law. Grace streams from one source which the human being with human strength cannot reach.

The Alpha and Omega One shall come. Spaceless time - timeless space. Everything is eternal, Holy now! The single-minded strength of Sagittarius must be used so that we can be capable of taking possession of the spiritual.

That which we have seen and received in the twelve Holy Nights, we have to carry into the material, spiritual and soul life. Rudolf Steiner

12. Heilige Nacht

4./5. Januar – Schütze

In der 12. Nacht wird die errungene Krone zu Füssen des Göttlichen niedergelegt, denn wir haben sie zwar selbst erkämpft, aber daß wir sie erringen durften ist Gnade, ist Gesetz des Geistigen. Denn Gnade ist Zustrom aus einer Quelle, die der Mensch mit menschlicher Kraft nicht zu erreichen vermag. Nun wird Anfang und Ende eines, raumlose Zeit – zeitloser Raum. Alles ist ewiges, heiliges Jetzt! Die zielstrebigen Kräfte des Schützen müssen so eingesetzt werden, daß er geistiges Gut in Empfang nehmen kann.

Das, was wir in den zwölf Heiligen Nächten erkannt und empfangen haben, müssen wir nun in das Leben hineintragen und die Materie und das Seelische durchgeistigen. Rudolf Steiner

Contemplations for the twelfth night by Kristina Kaine

Now we take our twelfth Holy Night step. These twelve steps which we have taken each day can become the theme for each month of the year ahead until we reach the renewal of our being at Christmas 2012.

We have contemplated our inner being and hopefully become more conscious of all the different activities that take place moment by moment within us. We have become more aware of the way our feelings rise up and can sweep us away if we do not intervene. Some of our thoughts that flit through our mind might have shocked us – they were always there we just don't notice them. Our impulses to act may also have become more conscious giving us the opportunity to assess our motives. At the very least, if we have become more aware of these three soul activities then we have experienced the highest in our being, our I Am.

Our I Am gives us poise and purpose, it changes the way we see our relationship to the world, and to all the people we encounter.

When we have those I Am experiences, we start to see Christ in every human being. The Cosmic Christ entered into this earth through the vehicle of Jesus and this spirit dwells in us. It dwells in us primarily through every breath we take and through the food we eat; food that is grown in the earth which is now the body of Christ. As we accept the reality of this, we begin to experience his etheric presence in the life-force of this earth and in our own etheric body. Now we begin to treat every person as if they were Christ. We arrest every negative thought before it forms because we see that we would be thinking that thought about Christ. We are careful about all our feelings and motives because of our respect for Christ in the other person. In this way, we transform ourselves and we raise the other person up as well. As St Paul said, "the glory of this mystery, which is Christ in you, the hope of glory." Colossians 1:27 If we did nothing else but contemplate this mystery each day through the year ahead we will change the world. 2012

~ ~ ~

Our crown is not for our own benefit. If we earn the crown, we place it at the feet of all creation. If we think it is our own crown, and that because we made the effort we should therefore reap the benefit, then we might be very surprised to one day discover who bestows these benefits.

The crown of humanity is the I AM and the essence of the I AM is love. "Love bears all things, believes all things, hopes all things, endures all things. Love never ends;" 1 Cor 13 When we experience this love we stand in the eternal "time without space and space out of time." This is the experience of the I AM. All boundaries disappear and we stand in our eternal being.

As we have travelled through these twelve Holy Nights, every glimpse of truth that has come to us has been received by the holy hierarchy and the divine trinity who hold us in their care. They receive our gifts of understanding and pour this out for all humanity. In these words we encounter the misunderstanding that as human beings we are beholden to God, or the gods. This is not true. We are free to earn the crown, wear the crown, and offer up the crown to the whole of creation. May we carry this knowledge through each day of the coming year. 2013

~ ~ ~

The crown is the sum total of our own accomplishments. What have we accomplished through these Holy Nights? What will we accomplish throughout the year ahead? This is the crown that we place at the foot of the Divine. As we strive to develop ourselves spiritually, it is not unusual to wonder just how much is required of us. At what point will we enter into the spiritual worlds having spiritualised ourselves sufficiently?

The pull towards the spiritual worlds is so strong in us that we must always be mindful that we must not wish to enter with any imperfections, any undeveloped human possibilities. It is enough for us to actually experience our soul and spiritual life while incarnated in this materialist world. In this way, we know our own value in the scheme of the cosmos. As esoteric Christians, this is our religion. As we grow in awareness of all the spiritual beings that support our efforts - the gods - we come to realise that we are their religion. They see our full potential and so should we. What the gods give us is dependent on what we have made of ourselves during each incarnation.

The Twelve Holy Nights assist us to focus on this task and guide us through the weeks and months ahead so that we can present ourselves to the gods at the end of the year so they can harvest what we have planted. 2014

~ ~ ~

What is "that source or fount in man that human power cannot reach?" Surely it is our I Am that is awakening the presence of Christ in our heart. This is the thinking heart, the heart that considers the importance of every thought knowing the effect that it will have on ourselves, on others and on the Universe.

Our journey through the 2014-15 Holy Nights has been one of realising just how much power we each have to change the world. It is within our power to spiritualise matter and to direct the soul's attention to all that is eternal. It is when we change ourselves that absolutely everything else changes.

If we choose to do only one thing throughout the year ahead, the one thing that will make the most impact, it is to suppress our opinions. In the Esoteric Classes held during the years 1904-1909 Rudolf Steiner had some very powerful words to say about the damage we cause when we express our opinions - not just to others but also privately to ourselves.

"When we succeed in holding back our own view, then we practice something of great significance and at the same time gain tremendous power. ... The more we are able to listen and not express our own opinion, the sooner we rise to immediate insight and direct spiritual sight. .... But in the same way that power is collected in a battery, we can collect forces in our souls when we suppress our opinions. It will result in inner power and strength." http://rudolfsteinerquotes.wordpress.com/2015/01/01/opinions-have-no-value-2/

Perhaps we can dedicate 2015 to 'The Year of No Opinions'. Then we earn the crown of the purity of will which we can lay at the foot of the Divine in us and everywhere. 2015

~ ~ ~

How often do we think about the assistance given to us when we apply spiritual truth in our lives? This is not necessarily 'God' granting our wishes or answering our prayer; this assistance comes to us from the ranks of the Spiritual Hierarchy who keep the whole Universe in order. It also comes from our Higher Self, our I AM as well as the presence of Christ in our hearts.

Sometimes we can think that applying spiritual principles in our lives is beyond us, and therefore it will be beyond us. However, if we say we can do it, and we demonstrate our willingness to do it, instantly we are assisted. If we notice some success with our endeavours, we should not be so quick to pat ourselves on the back for our achievement and forget to acknowledge the assistance. The word grace implies graciousness; our own graciousness for the grace we receive.

In the first Holy Night, we met the term Alpha and Omega when we considered the voice of silence. Now we meet it again, in the Omega of the Holy Nights. Three times we find these words Alpha and Omega in the Bible, all in The Revelation to John: 1:8, 21:6, and 22:13.

I quote from my book "The Soul's Secret Unveiled in the Book of Revelation Vol 1"*:

"'I am [ego eimi] the Alpha and the Omega,' says the Lord God, who is and who was and who is to come, the Almighty." Rev 1:8

"Ego eimi, the I AM, was in the beginning, was first (alpha) and is to come, that is, last (omega). This is not God, this is our own eternal being, our I AM. To fully understand all the implications of this we need knowledge of reincarnation and karma. It is this I AM that holds all our incarnations together like a string of pearls. The first pearl and the last pearl are all on the one string."

More than ever before this world needs those who stand in the power of their I AM. These Holy Nights have been a tender time, a time in which to reach out and touch eternity. This connection with our True Self, our Holy Self, will sustain us throughout the coming year. Thank you for travelling through the Holy Nights with me. 2016

*http://www.amazon.com/Souls-Secret-Unveiled-Revelation-Volume-ebook/dp/B00A96V50E 2016

THIRTEENTH HOLY NIGHT - EPIPHANY
January 5-6

Now we come to the thirteenth Holy Night. On the first Holy Night we celebrated the birth of Jesus. This birth awakened the deep memory within us of who we really are. It meant that we could touch the purity of our being as we were before we ever incarnated into a physical body. We have carried this memory in our heart through every incarnation on this earth. Twelve days ago we saw it lying there like a newborn.

Over these twelve nights and days, we have tended this tiny child, using our Imagination to nurture it, to give it life. Now we have arrived at the night when this child, that innocent memory within us, is ready to receive the Cosmic Christ. From the celestial sun on the wings of the holy dove comes this Christ we have yearned for through all the incarnations we have ever lived. Now Christ himself can be experienced within our being, this is our baptism, our Epiphany.

Do we really understand what it means to have the presence of the living Christ within us? On this night we have the opportunity to create a living Imagination of what this means for us. This journey over the last twelve days and nights, from Jesus to Christ, has changed us forever. We will carry our work in our hearts through the twelve months of the year that follows.

From the
THE HUMAN SOUL AND THE UNIVERSE
A lecture by Rudolf Steiner Berlin, February 20, 1917 GA 175

"Thus the peculiar sentiment we connect with the Mystery of Christmas and with its Festival is by no means arbitrary, but hangs together with the fixing of the Festival of Christmas. At that time in winter which is appointed for the Festival, man, as does indeed the whole earth, gives himself up to the Spirit. He then passes, as it were, through a realm in which the Spirit is near him. The consequence is that at about Christmas-time and on to our present New Year, man goes through a meeting of his astral body with the Life-Spirit, in the same way as he goes through the first meeting, that of his ego with the Spirit-Self.

Upon this meeting with the Life-Spirit depends the nearness of Christ Jesus. For Christ Jesus reveals Himself through the Life-Spirit. He reveals Himself through a being of the Realm of the Archangels. He is, of course, an immeasurably higher Being than they, but that is not the point with which we are concerned at the moment; what we have to consider is that He reveals Himself through a Being of the order of the Archangeloi. Thus through this meeting we draw specially near to Christ Jesus at the present stage of development — which has existed since the Mystery of Golgotha — and in a certain respect we may call the meeting with the Life-Spirit: the meeting with Christ Jesus in the very depths of our soul.

Now when a man either through developing Spiritual consciousness in the domain of religious meditation or exercises, or, to supplement these, has accepted the concepts and ideas of Spiritual Science, when he has thus deepened and spiritualized his life of impression and feeling, then, just as he can experience in his waking life the after-effects of the meeting with his Spirit-Self, so he will also experience the after-effects of the meeting with the Life-Spirit, or Christ.

It is actually a fact, my dear friends, that in the time following immediately on Christmas and up to Easter the conditions are particularly favourable for bringing to a man's consciousness this meeting with Christ Jesus. In a profound sense and this should not be blotted out by the abstract materialistic culture of today — the season of Christmas is connected with processes taking place in the earth; for man, together with the earth, takes part in the Christmas changes in the earth.

The season of Easter is determined by processes in the heavens. Easter Sunday is fixed for the first Sunday after the first full-moon after the Vernal Equinox. Thus, whereas Christmas is fixed by the conditions of the earth, Easter is determined from above. Just as we, through all that has just been described, are connected with the conditions of the earth, so are we connected, through what I shall now describe, with the conditions of the heavens — with the great Cosmic conditions.

For Easter is that season in the concrete course of the year, in which all that is aroused in us by the meeting with Christ at Christmas, really unites itself with our physical earth manhood. The great Mystery that now brings home to man the Mystery of Golgotha at the Easter Season — the Good Friday Mystery — signifies among other things, that the Christ, who, as it were, has been moving beside us, at this season comes still closer to us. Indeed, roughly speaking, in a sense He disappears into us and permeates us, so that He can remain with us during the season that follows the Mystery of Golgotha — the season of summer — during which, in the ancient Mysteries, men tried to unite themselves to John in a way not possible after the Mystery Of Golgotha.

- See more at:

http://wn.rsarchive.org/Lectures/19170220p02.html#sthash.XvOle5yH.dpuf

OTHER WORKS BY THE AUTHOR

Print publication

I Connecting : The Soul's Quest ISBN 978-0-9779825-3-0 published by Goldenstone Press July 2007

Published as an ebook in Kindle 2012 under the title "I AM The Mystery"

Workbook and workshop associated with this work: I AM Exercises published in 2013

Reflection series by Kristina Kaine

Kindle and Paperback

1. I AM The Soul's Heartbeat. Volume 1

The Seven I AM Sayings in St John's Gospel: 2003

2. I AM The Soul's Heartbeat. Volume 2

Christian Initiation in St John's Gospel: 2003 – 2004

3. I AM The Soul's Heartbeat. Volume 3

Finding the Eightfold Path of Buddha in St John's Gospel: 2004

4. I AM The Soul's Heartbeat. Volume 4

The Twelve Disciples in St John's Gospel: 2005

5. I AM The Soul's Heartbeat. Volume 5

The Seven Signs in St John's Gospel: 2006

6. I AM The Soul's Heartbeat. Volume 6

The Beatitudes in St John's Gospel: 2006 – 2007

7. The Soul's Secret Unveiled in the Book of Revelation: 2007 – 2010

2 volumes ebook, 1 volume print

Republished as The Virgin and The Harlot

1 volume ebook, 1 volume print

8. I AM The Soul's Heartbeat. Volume 7

9. The Bible Unlocked Blog: 2009 –

10. Who is Jesus : What is Christ : 2010 –

Published in volumes as the work is completed

Volume 1 June 2013

Volume 2 September 2013

Volume 3 June 2014

Volume 4 November, 2015

Volume 5 November 2016

11. I AM Exercises written with Anita-Joy Louis 2013

12. The Twelve Holy Nights November 2016

13. The Journey Back begun in October 2016

Kristina writes regularly about her understanding of the human soul and spirit.

You can read more of her work at the following websites.

http://www.facebook.com/EsotericConnection

http://www.esotericconnection.com/

http://www.soulquesting.net/

http://www.bibleunlocked.blogspot.com.au/

https://www.facebook.com/Spirit.SoulAwakening/

http://www.huffingtonpost.com/author/kristina-845

ABOUT THE AUTHOR

Kristina Kaine has worked with people all her life: during her early career in medical sales and staff recruitment, and for well over 20 years in her own business which matches people in business partnerships. Through this rich interaction with people, Kristina has observed the struggle for self identity from many angles. She was awakened to the ideas of Rudolf Steiner by Rev Mario Schoenmaker, attending all of Schoenmaker's lectures for 14 years.

After Schoenmaker's death in 1997, Kristina realized the need to explain the knowledge of the threefold human being in simple terms that could be applied easily in daily life. As well as her weekly Reflections that are read worldwide, she has set this out in her book, 'I Connecting : the Soul's Quest', which was published in 2007 by Robert Sardello. It is not unusual for her to receive comments about her book like this: "It seems like a very lucid treatment, like looking through a clear glass window through which one can discover and recognize the landscape of the soul."

Printed in Great Britain
by Amazon